CARNIVAL NOIR

CARNIVAL NOIR

RENE PIERRE

PELICAN PUBLISHING
New Orleans 2019

The word "Pelican" and the depiction of a pelican are
trademarks of Arcadia Publishing Company Inc. and are
registered in the U.S. Patent and Trademark Office.

Library of Congress Cataloging-in-Publication Data

Names: Pierre, Rene, author.
Title: Carnival noir / Rene Pierre.
Description: New Orleans, La. : Pelican Publishing, 2019. | Includes
  index.
Identifiers: LCCN 2018042429| ISBN 9781455622610 (hardcover : alk.
  paper) | ISBN 9781455622627 (ebook)
Subjects: LCSH: Carnival—Louisiana—New Orleans. | African
  Americans—Louisiana—New Orleans—Social life and customs. | New
  Orleans (La.)—Social life and customs. | Carnival—Louisiana—New
  Orleans—Pictorial works. | African Americans—Social life and
  customs—Louisiana—New Orleans—Pictorial works. | New Orleans
  (La.)—Social life and customs—Pictorial works.
Classification: LCC GT4211.N4 P54 2019 | DDC 394.2509763/35—dc23
LC record available at https://lccn.loc.gov/2018042429

Printed in the United States of America

Published by Pelican Publishing
New Orleans, LA
www.pelicanpub.com

CONTENTS

ACKNOWLEDGMENTS

I dedicate *Carnival Noir* to the late McKinnley Cantrell Sr. He was an inspiring and wonderful success story in the business of Mardi Gras. He built his empire with his own hands. His theory of "build it and they'll come" worked like a charm. I met him in 1996 through his son, McKinnley Jr. It was believed that his wife Beryl Cantrell was related to Miles Dutchman, of the Dutchman brothers, who built floats for the Babylon and Hermes parades, circa 1930.

Cantrell single-handedly introduced Las Vegas-style lighting to the carnival parades of New Orleans. After a trip to Sin City during the early 1970s, he became inspired by the illumination of the night scene there. As a result, he imported those ideas into building Mardi Gras floats. McKinley's zaniness and fun-spiritedness led him to invent some innovative art forms like lit secondary props and cutout decor for his floats. Like most Mardi Gras artists, he was always looking for the next big thing. Oddly enough, it was his wife who introduced the idea of the "throw cup" as we know of it today. At the time, the Cantrell family was a leader of the Metairie Krewe of Mardi Gras. Mrs. Beryl thought it would be a good idea to throw plastic cups with the krewe's logo affixed to it. In the krewe's first year, the cups were a hit. The crowds went crazy! Soon after, all krewes had adopted them as a part of their throw packages.

The Cantrells were also instrumental in jump-starting my current career in the Mardi Gras industry. While the Barth brothers gave me my first break, working on backgrounds for parade floats, it was the Cantrell family who offered me my first position as a detail artist. In this city, that is a true milestone for any young aspiring artist because of the tight-knit artist positions available. In addition, there were few African Americans doing so at the time. It was an exciting time in my life because of the opportunity.

McKinnley Cantrell Jr. (or Mac, as he was known) was the one who actually hired me to paint the Krewe of Babylon's floats for 1996. I was referred to Mac by Joe Barth Jr. He had turned down the Cantrell contract due to an overwhelming commission at Audubon Zoo and called me to pursue it. It was my fate to receive such a blessing. Mac Jr. was so impressed that he soon contacted his father to arrange a meeting with me. Mac Sr. was in search of an artist, too, since his previous artists had fled New Orleans to find other jobs elsewhere. I was offered the contract with both Cantrell partners.

This was a huge turning point in my art career. Mr. Cantrell Sr. was the nicest man I'd ever met. He treated his employees with respect and often treated them to delicious meals on many occasions. He tried to make work fun and comfortable for us all. His wittiness and kindness made it a joy to work for him. He worked in the studio in Kenner, Louisiana, up until his death in 2001. Since, I've cultivated long-lasting relationships with both his son and grandson, who I still do work for.

I am grateful to the Cantrell family for the inspirational role they have played in my career and for providing the training ground for my place and success in the Mardi Gras world as a professional artist.

INTRODUCTION

As a young boy, I've always been amazed by the size and glamour of the New Orleans Mardi Gras floats. It seemed striking like a Disney production of sort. While I cannot remember my grandfather hoisting me upon his shoulders, my mom invoked those memories through her compelling stories of yesteryear. The stories that impressed me most were her tales of Mardi Gras in the Negro neighborhoods. It was so captivating to hear of the beautiful Indian costumes and the motley Zulu parade at the time.

There were also memories of horror as she described scenes of her sisters and herself running and screaming at the Skeleton men—a group of black men dressed like skeletons, usually accompanying or leading the Indian tribes around town during Mardi Gras and St. Joseph's Day celebrations. Then, there were stories of the infamous picnic gatherings of families on N. Claiborne Avenue before the Interstate 10 was erected.

It was once a plush neutral ground laced with large leafy oak trees that served as the official site of parade watching for Negro families. Because segregation existed, black citizens were not allowed to travel to Canal Street to view parades. Nonetheless, some old timers have confirmed incidents of blacks on Canal Street for Mardi Gras and they never encountered any problems from the law nor other non-black citizens. It must have been the magic of Mardi Gras that would allow such tolerance.

My father knew more about the Zulu organization as he had family members who took part in their festivities. The Zulu parade at that time was unorganized and usually formed along Shakespeare Park uptown on Simon Bolivar Boulevard, then would make pit stops in front of their favorite barrooms. Floats would ride just about anywhere they wanted to.

These wonderful folk-style tales inspired me to write this book. The rich culture that manifests in New Orleans has had a direct impact on my career and life, as I also operate as a carnival artist, an organizer, and an historian. My passion for this unique city has driven me since youth to fully become consumed in it on many levels. I hope that you enjoy the stories as well as the vivid photos in this book and share it with loved ones and friends for years to come.

This book explores the early occurrences of African American participation in the New Orleans Mardi Gras. It goes without saying that this ethnic group has been very instrumental in how Carnival has been transformed and celebrated. Most of what we know is all handed down through generational stories. Most of these stories, although full of legend, remain true today. So many events and people have altered the state of Mardi Gras. From the evolution of parades and floats to the street marchers, we as natives have witnessed the numerous changes. A few were favored and some were frowned upon. As a forty-five-year-old artist, I witnessed a plethora of things and was told many stories. It is with pleasure that I leave you with this literature and pictorial story of how black America enveloped itself in the world's greatest free show—*Mardi Gras!*

CHAPTER 1

IN THE BEGINNING

New Orleans has long been a well sought-after city to visit. Its beautiful sky line, French Quarter, fine dining, and festivals set it apart from other American cities. At any time, one can walk down Bourbon Street and hear pulsating jazz pumping from the row of clubs that exist. In the same breath, you can also witness a street parade or jazz funeral that locals call a second line.

The name comes from how the second lines are arranged. The funeral mourners were the first line in the street procession and the next group of dancers were known as the second line. According to stories of old, shared by my late grandmother and a host of deceased uncles, the Skeleton and Baby Doll groups followed by the Mardi Gras Indians were the main attractions for onlookers.

Story being told, the jazz bands that usually played for funerals would come out on Mardi Gras day and get people to follow them from bar room to bar room. They would stop along the way to drink and be merry. It was also told that most of the Baby Dolls were the street women of the night. They would be adorned in colorful satin clothing that resembled bedtime wear. The women also had a raunchy style of dance that they would do behind the second-line bands.

The Skeleton groups were really an adjunct to the Indians. The Skeletons ran wild through the housing developments and scared young children with their handmade masks and costumes. These groups were founded around the same time as the Indians. Skeletons would travel early in the morning on Mardi Gras before the Indians to strike fear into all who dared to embrace them. Many of them carried actual cow bones and deer antlers to add a kind of realistic appeal. Their handmade costumes consisted of dyed long johns sleepwear or undergarments, black shoes, and gloves that were decorated with skeletal bones drawn using white shoe polish. Some men used white house paint to decorate their costumes.

These groups continue to march in current Carnival celebrations. The

Skeletons annually display and speak about their tradition at the New Orleans Jazz and Heritage Festival. Their handcrafted papier-mâché head masks are an attraction for many tourists who are curious to know about their role in Mardi Gras.

Because of segregation laws of the time, black citizens were not permitted to patronize Canal Street so they kept to their own neighborhoods. The main thoroughfare African Americans used to celebrate Mardi Gras was Basin Street and Orleans Avenue. Families also utilized N. Claiborne Avenue as a convenient picnic area for the day. To embellish upon the locations, we need to discuss N. Claiborne Avenue pre-I-10 as the official grounds for partying.

Many, if not all, Creole and African American families gathered on the neutral ground between St. Bernard Avenue and Orleans Avenue. The N. Claiborne corridor between St. Bernard Avenue and Bienville Street served

Theodore Emile "Bo" Dollis Sr., Big Chief of the Wild Magnolias, asks his assistant to adjust his crown before heading out to the Mardi Gras route. (Photographer unknown, photo courtesy of Gerard "Bo" Dollis Jr.)

Gerard "Bo" Dollis Jr., Big Chief of the Wild Magnolias tribe, masks during 2013 New Orleans Jazz Fest. (Photographer unknown, photo courtesy of Gerard "Bo" Dollis Jr.)

Bo Dollis Jr. sports his new beaded panels before heading out to his Mardi Gras route. (Photographer unknown, photo courtesy of Gerard "Bo" Dollis Jr.)

An Indian dances with the crowd during Mardi Gras. (Photograph by Rene Pierre)

New Orleans Indians sing and dance with the Carnival crowd near the interstate in 1970. (Photograph by Milton Pierre)

as the official grounds for partying amongst African Americans. Canal Street was off limits to people of color due to old Jim Crow laws, which made the corridor perfect for the community. Families would gather on the lush green space and stage picnics or barbeque all day. It was a front-row seat for the spectacle that was sure to pass by. The black community was able to celebrate to the fullest extent in costume.

Back then, just about everyone wore costumes. Presently, the younger generation has retired that tradition in favor of fancy expensive jeans and sneakers. This could be attributed to young parents not passing down the practice of costuming. This is almost like losing a native language. Many families would dress out in large groups, either in the same costumes or coordinating outfits. Store-bought costumes were often too expensive and out of reach for large families, so it was tradition that everyone wore a hand-sewn costume. Handmade costumes allowed everyone the ability to mask on Mardi Gras. Many housewives were also seamstresses either professionally or unprofessionally. This meant many mothers and grandmothers sewed costumes for their family members, especially the children. Unlike the Indians, who took about a year to make their creations, the children's costumes only took a day or week at best to prepare. This costume tradition was so in vogue to the point that schoolchildren would often discuss what they'd planned to wear on Fat Tuesday.

Bo Dollis Jr. sports his new digs for Mardi Gras. (Photographer unknown, photo courtesy of Gerard "Bo" Dollis Jr.)

This young Indian's costume takes center stage in a 1969 family photo. A lot of detail and hard work goes into Mardi Gras costumes, no matter the size. (Photograph by Milton Pierre)

Young New Orleans Indians masking during Mardi Gras of 1969. (Photograph by Milton Pierre)

A young Indian shows off their costume in 1969.
(Photograph by Milton Pierre)

During Mardi Gras of 1969, a young Indian dances in full costume. (Photograph by Milton Pierre)

A young Indian dances during the 1968 Carnival season. (Photograph by Milton Pierre)

Whether you bought it or made it at home, you had to have a costume or a mask. Back then, no one would be caught without a costume. This was in contrast to modern attire of new blue jeans and t-shirts. Costuming added more fun to the existing merriment of Mardi Gras. In addition to costuming, African American families also explored the joy of riding on floats by creating their own individual clubs.

These clubs usually consisted of families and close friends. While the all-white trucking clubs were rolling uptown, the black neighborhoods produced their own truck floats and rode in and around the Tremé and Seventh Ward areas. A few families who could afford it built and decorated truck floats, which they would ride around the neighborhood, throwing all sorts of goodies. Throws of the period weren't as fancy as we know them now. Because there weren't throw supply companies around or rules as strict as today's, krewes threw pretty much whatever they wanted to. Throws would include toys, flowers, food items such as fruit and vegetables, and even articles of clothing.

The black trucking clubs enjoyed parading around just about anywhere they wanted to since permits weren't needed for single-riding truck floats. As time passed and Carnival activities grew, the laws began to change as it pertains to crowd control and parading. Those laws that granted stricter requests of parading trucks forced the black truckers to join the ranks of established trucking krewes, which were predominately white. The African American celebration virtually went untouched for years except for Zulu, which was granted a parade permit in 1971. That one permit landed them on St. Charles Avenue and Canal Street. That was uncharted territory for black folks during Carnival. The Indians, Skeleton groups, and other marching groups paraded as usual since none of them needed parade permits to do their thing. The absence of the black truckers and the building of I-10 in the '60s changed the very fabric of Carnival celebration scenes in those neighborhoods. Current revelers now use the I-10 as a shelter to escape rainy conditions and as a place to sell wares, food, and, of course, party. The Mardi Gras Indians often meet up there, as well as the Skeleton groups.

The Indians as we currently know them in New Orleans really don't like to be classified as Mardi Gras Indians. They're just simply, New Orleans Indians. It is noted that these Indians started their tradition as far back as 200 years ago. Supposedly, there were laws on the book that prevented blacks from dancing in the streets with feathers. Some believe that the New Orleans Indians became so as a result of gratitude to the Native Americans of Louisiana who helped slaves find their way to freedom. Local native reservations were a safe haven for slaves and plantation masters were prohibited by law from stepping foot on the grounds uninvited.

Joe "Sabu" Thomas, member of the Yellow Pocahontas tribe, dances in the street during Mardi Gras in the '60s. Masking during Mardi Gras is a unique New Orleans tradition that's been passed from generation to generation. (Photograph by Milton Pierre)

New Orleans Indian Joe "Sabu" Thomas with another Indian and Mardi Gras reveler in the '60s. (Photograph by Milton Pierre)

A New Orleans Indian's costume is on full display during Carnival season.
(Photograph by Rene Pierre)

A New Orleans Indian shows off the detailed patchwork on the back of his costume. (Photograph by Rene Pierre)

At the time blacks were celebrating, Louisiana was not yet a part of the American Union. They were reveling with people indigenous to the area. Some black citizens were not imported through the African slave trade. They came through other means and from other countries, such as the Caribbean islands.

Under the guise of celebrating European holidays, blacks found a way to mask without recourse. Those holidays were familiar to them, which is why they were chosen. Carnival season was the time they chose to dress and revel in the streets because it was legal. Celebrating during other European festivities encouraged them to mask on holidays besides Mardi

Gras, which led to the namesake being New Orleans Indians and not Mardi Gras Indians.

More tribes developed and were meeting each other with competition. During the nineteenth century celebrations, it was noted that tribes would fire rifles as warning signals that another tribe was close by. The masking idea also spawned the notion of retaliation of violence that transpired during the year amongst peers, hence the old saying *"I know you Mardi Gras."* That phrase, if said to you, meant that the other person masked was going to get you (violently) on that day as a means of getting away with it.

When masking, Indians were usually accompanied by drummers who ushered them through the streets. Their tradition and culture was cultivated, practiced, and handed down to younger generations. As time persisted, Indian costumes, as well as some practices, experienced a paradigm shift.

A spy boy makes way for the chief and the rest of the tribe to come through under the Claiborne Avenue Bridge. (Photographer unknown, photo courtesy of Gerard "Bo" Dollis Jr.)

A New Orleans Indian, Demond Peters, stands out in a crowd of Mardi Gras revelers. (Photograph by Rene Pierre)

A New Orleans Indian celebrates in the streets during the 1969 Mardi Gras season. (Photograph by Milton Pierre)

A New Orleans Indian is a show-stopper (and traffic-stopper) as he masks during Mardi Gras of 1969. (Photograph by Milton Pierre)

The young people being reared in this culture also have a responsibility of learning about it. At one time there was a fear of losing it due to family breakdowns over recent years and loss of interest. But present times show a healthy participation of young people getting involved as to preserve something that's very near and dear to our hearts. Older Indians have been handing down this tradition for years and younger generations have added to it. Some new trends introduced by the younger ones include LED lighting in the headdresses or crowns and 3-D formed aprons and crowns. It's easy to say that the New Orleans Indian tradition will always be a permanent piece of our celebration.

Costumes generally consisted of satin, stones, feathers, and ribbons. Different tribes dawned different styles. Uptown Indians wear more ostrich plumes and velvet, whereas downtown ones wore more marabou and turkey feathers. The most famous chief, Tootie Montana, truly changed the way Indians dress and meet each other.

Allison "Tootie" Montana, Big Chief of the Yellow Pocahontas tribe, single handedly introduced the three-dimensional costume features in addition to the way Indians met each other. In earlier times, most tribes often met with violence like the firing of rifles. However, Tootie's theory was to channel the animosity into competing with beauty. It worked like a charm. Competition quickly replaced the traditions of the old wild scenes. Indians now do dances and express languages only known to each other. Costumes have become larger, prettier, brighter, and cladded with more features. According to Gerard "Bo" Dollis Jr., downtown tribes trimmed their patches with black beads and the uptown tribes trimmed theirs with white beads. This is how one was able to tell them apart.

The problem with outside cultures understanding this particular culture is that the wrong information about the Indians was being presented to the public at large. The New Orleans Indians have suffered some exploitation over the years from outsiders, which is why a lack of cooperation with many Mardi Gras projects existed. Most Indians aren't going to exchange information with those who have no vested interest in the culture. As a people who live and breathe the tradition, there comes an understanding of solidarity.

Likeminded people usually hobnob with one another and so it is that the local Indian culture would be more cooperative with their own kind. Tootie Montana fought for the rights of the New Orleans Indian culture up until his death. After being pressured by police in a St. Joseph parade, he and other chiefs who sat on the board for the Mardi Gras Indian Association met with councilmembers and New Orleans Police Department officials at City Hall. During this meeting Tootie suffered a heart attack, probably due to the stress of pleading his rights. There was another meeting at the Mahalia Jackson Theater that also preempted the City Hall meeting. The city and the Indians finally came to an amicable agreement as it referred to street parading and the police understanding their culture. It was a shame that Tootie could not live to see its fruition.

It was only a matter of time before city officials passed legislature to force free-riding trucks to join already organized parading organizations. One of the first African American truck-float clubs to join an existing all white organization was the Baudi family in Gentilly. According to them, they were met with some opposition but not quite enough to keep them away. As a sign of the times, more black truck clubs followed and trucking organizations became fully integrated. The late '70s and mid '80s saw the onslaught of many changes to that effect.

The Ernest "Dutch" Morial administration witnessed major changes of how Mardi Gras would be celebrated. The late '70s involved a police strike that left many parading krewes lifeless. The '80s brought on the dissipation of many new krewes due to the oil bust. However, African Americans virtually went untouched. The Indians, Skeletons, and black truck-float clubs paraded as usual since none of them needed official permits to parade. While second-line clubs and the aforementioned marching groups were still doing their thing on foot, the discontinuation of the black truck floats put a damper on the Claiborne Avenue spirit since that was the gathering area for African Americans. It was already bad enough that the Interstate 10 was constructed through there to alter the natural state of things. It is rumored that there are plans to reroute the I-10 around that area to bring back the neutral grounds and lush trees to face Claiborne Avenue.

Where the newly built extension would travel has not been discussed

Big Chief Merk pays his respects at Allison "Tootie" Montana's 2005 funeral. Tootie was—and remains—an influential part of New Orleans's Mardi Gras culture. (Photograph by Rene Pierre)

*Big Chief Merk in full costume at Tootie Montana's
funeral in 2005.* (Photograph by Rene Pierre)

Big Chief Merk in 2005 at Tootie Montana's funeral. (Photograph by Rene Pierre)

A New Orleans officer gladly poses for a photo as he's escorts (and enjoys) the Zulu parade. The NOPD has played a crucial role in keeping the peace and taming the chaos of Mardi Gras. (Photograph by Rene Pierre)

publicly. Post construction of the I-10 in the '60s, some folks used it as a convenient covered stage area to set up DJ booths and live concerts that would survive any weather. This allowed for a good time on the avenue, no matter if there was rain, sleet, or (the rare) snow. In current times, Mardi Gras day on Claiborne Avenue seems and feels more like a mini Jazz Fest. The underside of the I-10 is now laced with food and art vendors. There are also temporary photo studios set up in the back of box vans to allow for fun photos on the go for a fee. Many of the bar rooms and other establishments in that area throw parties and sell food and beverages that day to keen in on extra capital. The Zulu parade passes through the Basin Street area annually, adding more merriment to the spirit of things.

Even though many African Americans don't mask anymore, there are still old terms of endearment or not, still remembered by our old-timers. The most popular of them is "I know *you* Mardi Gras!" That meant I've identified you as a person but you don't know me because of my disguise. Some people used that as a threatening term, meaning "I'm going to get you later for the things you've done to me in the past." The Indians used to fire rifles as a way of warning other tribes not to mess with them. Most tribes had Spy Boys, Flag Boys, and Wild Men. Each played a role in the protection of the tribes. Tribes went through long kept rituals to pass each other in crossing from one part of town to another. These performances are usually dramatic and are a sight to see.

One Indian chief, who really sparked a change in the volatile type of challenges into one of a competition of beauty was Allison "Tootie" Montana, the chief of the Yellow Pocahontas. He was later given the name Big Chief. In his own rite, he became the ambassador for all Indians in New Orleans. In addition to the Indian and Skeleton groups, there were other zany elements throughout that same neighborhood that contributed to more revelry, such as the town drunkards dressed in drag. The drag queens added to very funny sideshows for pedestrians to laugh at. These men would garb in tacky old women's clothing and hand-me-down beat-up wigs, holding onto their last swig of spirits. It was hilarious to see!

The Mardi Gras scene in the African American neighborhoods has really changed. Younger generations are struggling to keep old traditions alive and keep the Carnival atmosphere safe and friendly. Unfortunately, some intruders get off on causing tragedy and mishaps. Local law enforcement agents work hard and diligently every year to curtail such behavior to ensure a pleasurable family environment. The Indians hold special practice all year long in their neighborhoods to keep young people involved and off the streets. Smaller float builders offer young art students opportunities to work under professional artists to keep them earning honorable money and out of harm's way. Other community centers offer special workshops for young ones to learn about their culture as it pertains to Mardi Gras. It is with much hope that the coming generation learns enough cultural knowledge to pass the torch along.

CHAPTER 2

ZULU NATION

One of the most famous organizations in all of Mardi Gras is the Zulu club. The Zulu organization is one of the largest Mardi Gras krewes of the African American community. It got its start as a group of workingmen trying to help each other. Prior to the '50s, most insurance companies wrote very few policies for Negro citizens. So it was common that groups of men pooled their funds to bury each other because they couldn't afford life insurance. A few men from one group circa 1909 attended a vaudeville play, which was popular at the time since movie theaters were not yet invented. The play was named *There Never Was and Never Will Be a King Like Me.* It featured black men in black face mimicking the king of the Zulus in Africa. The men were moved by it and named their club after it. The name has been embedded in the history of Carnival ever since.

The official name of the organization that stages the Zulu parade is the Zulu Social Aid and Pleasure Club, Inc. Around the early twentieth century, Zulu never had a planned parade route. In fact, it stayed that way up until the very late '60s. They would just ride on old garbage wagons decorated with moss, hay, and palmetto leaves. The krewe would wear old burlap sacks, grass skirts, and other things to look like Zulu warriors. The parade used to travel from barroom to barroom stopping at each one to celebrate. It was unorganized but fun. The black community would create a huge following behind the parade in hopes of landing a treasured coconut. Hence, the Zulu coconut is one the most popular throws in all of Mardi Gras.

Coconuts, according to Zulu historians, represented pieces of gold, silver, and ore. It is rare to see silver ones now. However, the gold and black ones remain popular. After Zulu suffered several lawsuits in the late '80s and '90s, the club decided to incorporate plastic coconuts, which were not well-received. The krewe was ultimately able to purchase gutted coconuts that were pre-painted. These were a lot lighter and less costly but were the real thing. A law was also passed that the krewe could only hand these

The standard-bearer leads the 1989 Zulu parade. The banner behind him displays the full name of the organization and its motto "The pride of the Crescent City." (Photograph by Milton Pierre)

A duke rolls through the streets in the Zulu parade of 1978. (Photograph by Milton Pierre)

A Zulu duke has a prime seat on the back of a convertible in the 1978 parade. (Photograph by Milton Pierre)

A Zulu duke is accompanied by a younger crowned member during the 1978 parade. (Photograph by Milton Pierre)

coconuts out from the lower levels of huge double-decked floats. It was all a part of promoting a safer ride with fewer threats of litigation.

Another rarity is the role of the Zulu queen. Because the early twentieth century presented itself with many chauvinistic practices and customs in America, women were not welcomed to be a krewe member. In one instance a neighborhood drag queen named Corrine played the part of queen for Zulu. Its first king was William Story, who wore a lard can crown and held a banana stalk as a scepter. The Zulus accompanying him wore old cut up rags with black face makeup and wooly wigs. They didn't ride floats until later in the century, around the early 1950s. Garbage wagons decorated with palmetto leaves were the first floats.

With a sparkling crown and scepter in hand, Queen Zulu greets the crowd in 1981. (Photograph by Milton Pierre)

The 1981 Zulu queen is joined by a younger member of the court as she greets the crowd of paradegoers. (Photograph by Milton Pierre)

The Queen Zulu float prepares to join the parade of 1989. (Photograph by Milton Pierre)

The colorful Zulu queen of 1989 greets the crowd from her throne. (Photograph by Milton Pierre)

The king of Zulu proudly sits on his thrown on a float adorned with the king of the jungle. (Photograph by Milton Pierre)

King Zulu, Elliot Bottiere, stands proudly on his majestic float as he greets the crowd during the parade of 1981. (Photograph by Milton Pierre)

The king of Zulu greets the crowd during the krewe's 1986 parade. (Photograph by Milton Pierre)

King Zulu of 1989 greets a crowd of paradegoers in front of the Tremé Supermarket. (Photograph by Milton Pierre)

Zulu warriors stand fiercely with pride above the crowd of onlookers in 2007.
(Photograph by Milton Pierre)

The duchesses of 2004 pose for a photo at the Zulu Character Party. (Photograph
by Rene Pierre)

A pair of dukes show off their bright and intricate costumes for the 2004 Zulu parade. (Photograph by Milton Pierre)

Along with the civil rights movement, the '60s spawned significant changes in New Orleans, including the integration of Canal Street. Suddenly, all citizens were welcome to enjoy the festivity of Canal Street, which was a major thoroughfare of Mardi Gras. Upon integration, there weren't any major incidents reported. This event gave way to Zulu requesting a standard parade route. Many citizens became leery of this move made by the organization, fearing that it would cause political unrest, riots, and pandemonium. It worked out to be a sweet merger. One great irony of Mardi Gras is how—in a southern city such as this—various ethnicities can come together for the sake of having a good time. It is an understood behavior that comes naturally every year. There is low to no civil crime, all ethnic groups get along and young and old alike convene to enjoy a season of merriment. This is a controlled chaos, to say the least. The '60s also saw Zulu go through its own political upheavals.

The newer, younger members of the organization found themselves fighting a new battle against the older ones when it came to black men wearing blackface. Remember that black men doing vaudeville shows in the 1920s was acceptable in its time. It didn't rest well with the more educated youth who were on the frontlines of the civil rights movement. Although they put up a good fight to end blackface in Zulu and even threatened to boycott the club, it remained that the members should continue the blackface tradition. It's believed that the late Jim Russell contributed largely to regaining peace among members. Zulu enjoyed an influx of many young urban professionals as more and more black youth were earning college degrees and landing higher paying jobs. In addition, it opened its ridership to women and non-black citizens. Zulu grew into a superkrewe very fast, especially under the leadership of the late Jim Russell—who was one of the oldest living members, and even rode with Louis Armstrong when the musician was king. He along with members like Morris Jeff, Roy Glapion, Clarence Becknell, Milton Behenemy, Cyrus Cagnolatti, and a host of other fine young men of the era helped shape Zulu into the krewe we see on the streets today.

A duke enjoys the ride in a convertible during the Zulu parade of 1978. (Photograph by Milton Pierre)

The Blaine Kern family currently provides the floats for Zulu through a rental contract. Before the Kern Companies' involvement, it was believed that there was a member by the name of Lucian Barbarian who built the krewe's floats. Prior to the 1950s, floats were built over old garbage wagons. They were usually not a permanent fixture as they were decorated with moss, hay, and palmetto leaves—the natural décor helped simulate the krewe's realistic tribal environment theme. It is in the air that this could change real soon, too, as the krewe is steadily finding ways to build their own floats. That rumor is a long awaited and welcomed change. However, it's easier said than done. Building floats can be very expensive but is always more cost-effective through self-building efforts and ownership of a storage space in the long run. If it ever came to pass that Zulu pulled off such a program, it is almost guaranteed that their floats would outdo all of its rival parades. This parade draws immeasurable crowds in search of a roaring good time. Zulu has the most marching bands besides Endymion. They offer the most variety of throws, including that prized coconut. Zulu also has many novelty features like their walking groups, the old gold fire engine, their splendid dukes and duchesses, and marching puppets.

Paradegoers in 2002 try to get the attention of the Zulu krewe in order to get one of the unique throws. (Photograph by Milton Pierre)

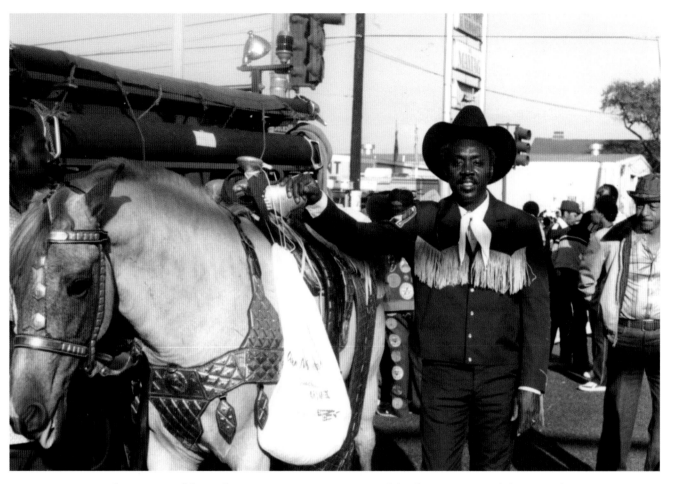

A horseman of the Zulu equestrian team poses with his horse in 1987. (Photograph by Milton Pierre)

Witchress Ann Cagnolatti stands on the top deck of a float in the 1990 Zulu parade. (Photograph by Milton Pierre)

Zulu maids greet the crowd during the 2002 parade. (Photograph by Milton Pierre)

A duke prepares to roll in the Zulu parade of 1979. (Photograph by Milton Pierre)

In 2003 Zulu commissioned my company, Crescent City Artists, to provide the walking papier-mâché heads. That is one lost art and feature of the Mardi Gras that should return. The papier-mâché walking heads were the first costumes used in Mardi Gras. The Krewe of Comus ushered the tradition in during the late nineteenth century. They were beautifully done and poked fun at local politicians. As funny as they were, their larger than life size were feared by children. Today, children welcome them as it is reminiscent of Disney characters. Unfortunately, the Katrina disaster caused a devastating loss of the papier-mâché sculptures.

The Zulu krewe's day starts extremely early. The entire krewe meets at the New Orleans Hilton Hotel to prep for the parade at 5 a.m. where costumes, make-up, and headgear are distributed. This is also an opportunity for krewe members to indulge in an extravagant breakfast, including alcohol-based breakfast drinks. The members are then transported to the floats parked at the Superdome for boarding. It is protocol that throws be loaded on the floats the night before the actual parade as to not cause a fiasco on Mardi Gras day. This phase of prep has worked well since Zulu has been notorious for tardiness in the past. The filled floats are then escorted to the formation area located at S. Claiborne and Jackson avenues. The latter was included upon the new Canal Street route change in the '60s because the owners of Gertrude Geddes' funeral home—which is located on Jackson Avenue—were sponsors of the parade for quite some time during the days of unorganized parading. In addition to its parade, the Zulu ball is an amazing star-studded event.

Krewe members prepare for the 2006 Zulu parade. (Photograph by Rene Pierre)

A Zulu duke shows off his costume before the 1983 parade. (Photograph by Milton Pierre)

Krewe members relaxing after the 1986 Zulu parade. (Photograph by Milton Pierre)

Their ball can boast up to 15,000 patrons, including well-known musicians and movie stars. The court is usually presented in the early evening hours to reserve time for a major concert that takes place well into the night and following morning. There is also the biggest second line you'd ever want to see. The Zulu ball is a well sought-after invite. Having the privilege of being invited to their ball is a true honor. However, well gone are the days of the free invites to the ball. It has largely become commercialized through the sale of tables to the general public. These sales have helped the ball become a thriving fundraiser in the likes of its other superkrewe neighbors. Anyone with money and the desire to attend can purchase tables of ten from the krewe's headquarters. The balls have always been known for the high-ranked acts like Chaka Khan, The Isley Brothers, Keith Sweat, The O'Jays, Babyface Edmonds, and Frankie Beverly and Maze. This one event has bloated in size over the years. During the days of the Rivergate's existence, the Zulu ball was much smaller and still held an amazing 3,000 people. The acts were mainly local but stunning and fun.

Actor Danny Glover prepares to throw a cup to the crowd of Zulu's 1989 parade. Glover served as the krewe's grand marshal. (Photograph by Milton Pierre)

A ticket for the Zulu 2009 Coronation Ball. The Zulu ball has a strict dress code for the star-studded event, which tends to end early the next morning. (Photograph by Rene Pierre)

The Zulu organization also presents debutantes, introducing the young ladies to society, like other elite clubs. They are presented in grand fashion with beautiful evening gowns and gorgeous headdresses. Each young lady is sponsored by their parents or guardians who wish to splurge in having their daughters participate in this occasion. It's not uncommon that this endeavor can reach an astronomical cost.

Zulu has come a long way from its first parading efforts. It has made indelible marks in the history of Mardi Gras. One of the most famous kings was Louis "Satchmo" Armstrong. Thought to be the father of jazz, he was New Orleans's most famous and prolific musician. Louis drew such a crowd that it landed his float on the curbside totally destroyed because everyone wanted a piece of it as a memorabilia. It created national attention. It even landed his face on the front page of *Time* magazine. Zulu has kept this treasured memory in its recorded history books. So no wonder everyone wanted to be a part of it. While this body of information only touches upon what we do know about the Zulu organization, there is still a plethora of stories still stuck in the minds of many who have experienced and/or witnessed the unsung adventures. That, in itself, is the making of another book.

Krewe of Zulu president, the late Roy Glapion, greets members during the 1989 parade. (Photograph by Milton Pierre)

*Rolling down Canal Street in front of the Saenger Theater, Desiree Glapion—
the queen of Zulu and daughter of the late Roy Glapion—greets the crowd of
paradegoers.* (Photograph by Milton Pierre)

Mardi Gras artist Rene Pierre and his father, Milton, pose with the Zulu poster for 2005. (Photographer unknown)

The proposed Zulu poster for 2009 celebrates the 100th anniversary of the krewe.
(Photograph by Milton Pierre)

A pair of krewe members smile for a picture during the 1983 float parade.
(Photograph by Milton Pierre)

Members of Zulu on a float during a 1984 parade. (Photograph by Milton Pierre)

Krewe members "take flight" on their float during the 1987 Zulu parade.
(Photograph by Milton Pierre)

Zulu krewe members greet the crowd during Mardi Gras of 1987. (Photograph by Milton Pierre)

Float for the Krewe of Zulu rolls during Mardi Gras of 1989. (Photograph by Milton Pierre)

The soulful warriors throw treats to the crowd during the Zulu parade of 2002.
(Photograph by Milton Pierre)

CHAPTER 3

AFRICAN AMERICAN CARNIVAL CLUBS

Zulu wasn't the only African American organization that enjoyed its roots in early Carnival. There were several old-line Carnival organizations within the black community that were fledging and still exist in this century of merrymaking. The Original Illinois Club, started by a successful Chicago businessman, remains one of the most elite clubs in town. Included in that lineup would be: the Young Men of Illinois, the Exclusive Twenties, the Capetowners, the Beaux Brummels, the Vikings, the Black Pirates, the Plantation Revelers, the Arelius Zuluranians, and a few others. Other parading organizations include: the successful and large Krewe of Nomtoc; the short-lived Krewe of Ashanti; its protégé Oshun, which is still in existence; and the more recently founded Krewe of Athena and the Mystic Krewe of Femme Fatale.

The first royal couple of Ashanti, crowned queen Ann Cagnolatti and crowned king Chester Pichon, are presented during the krewe's inaugural ball. (Photograph by Milton Pierre)

Her majesty the first Ashanti Queen Mother, Ann Cagnolatti, sits on her thrown in the krewe's 1993 inaugural parade. (Photograph by Milton Pierre)

The Krewe of Oshun went all-out decorating the floats for their first parade in 1997. (Photograph by Rene Pierre)

The floats for the Krewe of Oshun lineup before the krewe's 1997 inaugural parade. (Photograph by Rene Pierre)

The Original Illinois Club was the grandfather to all high-society organizations of African American descent. According to members, a Pullman porter named Wiley Knight started the prestigious organization. He worked on railroads in Chicago, Illinois, that ran directly to New Orleans. Wiley met an affluent family from New Orleans while at the Columbian Exposition of 1894. After being impressed by him, the family offered him employment in New Orleans. He accepted it and relocated here.

Wiley noticed a need for social grace in the Negro community and thus opened a dance school to teach such things. The first ball was held at Globe Hall, located at St. Peter and Marais streets. The dance-school group quickly formed into a club and adorned the name Illinois Club due to most members' original geographical area of residence. Though founded by a man, the first president was a woman—Ms. Louise Fortier. She would also become the club's first queen. The Original Illinois Club also presented debutantes. These young ladies are known to go through six months of training, which included classes in etiquette.

An admit card for the Original Illinois Club's ball. (Photograph by Rene Pierre)

The Original Illinois Club

request the honor of your company

to view

The Debutante Cotillion

at its

113ᵗʰ Annual Carnival Ball

Saturday, the twenty second of February

Two thousand and fourteen

Seven thirty of the clock

The New Orleans Event and Film Studio

233 Newton Street

New Orleans, Louisiana

Attire:

Ladies: Long formal gowns – no evening pants

Men: Black tie tuxedoes or white tails

An invitation to the Original Illinois Club's 2014 Carnival ball. (Photograph by Rene Pierre)

A warrior for the Original Illinois Club is in full uniform. (Photograph by)

1965 Queen and Court

Queen
Miss Joan Duplynn Rhodes

Science Major, Dillard, University. Daughter of
Mr. and Mrs. Duplain W. Rhodes, Jr., of New
Orleans.

The Original Illinois Club's queen for 1965, Miss Joan Duplynn Rhodes, featured in the krewe's program. (Photographer unknown)

1965 Debutantes

Miss Katherine Elizabeth Diggs. Senior, George Washington Carver Senior High School. Daughter of Mr. and Mrs. Alfred Diggs of New Orleans.

Miss Patricia Ann Knatt. Student, Dillard University, Elementary Education Major. Daughter of Mr. and Mrs. Arthur Joseph Knatt, Sr. of New Orleans.

Miss Diane Bernadette Le-Cesne. Elementary Education Major, Xavier University. Daughter of Mr. and Mrs. Armond LeCesne of New Orleans.

Miss Sylvia Wilhelmina Jones. Foreign Language Major, University of Southwestern Louisiana. Daughter of Mr. and Mrs. Randolph Jones of Natchitoches, La.

Miss Jo Ann Nicholas. Physical Education Major, Dillard University. Daughter of Mr. and Mrs. Geo. W. Nicholas Sr. of New Orleans.

Miss Wanda Lee Rouzan. Senior, Xavier Preparatory. Daughter of Mr. and Mrs. Harold S. Rouzan of New Orleans.

Debutantes of the Original Illinois Club's 1965 court. (Photograph by Rene Pierre)

During the ball for the Original Illinois Club, the king—accompanied by pages—makes his debut. (Photographer unknown)

Debutantes are presented at the ball for the Original Illinois Club. (Photographer unknown)

Wiley Knight attended his last ball in 1941. He passed around 1953. Kenneth Johnston is the longest active member, having been in place for forty-one years. EJ Roberts, of Gulfport, Mississippi, currently serves as the president. The growth of the club and expansion of ball activities has made it necessary for the club to move its festivities from the now-defunct Municipal Auditorium to the Ernest N. Morial Convention Center.

Parading organizations are much tougher to start and manage due to the large number of members it takes to keep the hefty cash flow running to operate the events and activities. It still remains a mystery that the Zulu organization only owns two of the many floats it uses. However, keep in mind that the Zulu organization's name includes "Social Aid and Pleasure Club" and the group is not really a krewe. Thus, the priority of its street pageantry may tend to be different from other superkrewes.

Other organizations are forced to rent floats from local companies to stay within certain budgets. The Krewe of Ashanti suffered its loss due to low budgets that stunt the growth and expansion of its organization. It also suffered a lot of internal conflict, which caused the demise of the organization. Ashanti could have been a fledgling and wealthy enough organization to compete with the likes of the Krewe of Orpheus. Although the krewe didn't last long, it did manage to set some new standards. The wearing of the kufi (African head gear) by kings in downtime was started by Ashanti. So was the ushering in of a king and queen at its coronation by an African drum corps, which became a standard in Zulu. Most citizens don't realize that Ashanti started that particular tradition.

The court of Ashanti is presented during the coronation ball. The splendor of the krewe's inaugural ball provided much inspiration for other krewes. (Photograph by Milton Pierre)

The royal court of the Krewe of Ashanti is presented during the 1993 inaugural coronation ball. (Photograph by Milton Pierre)

The first queen and king of the Krewe of Ashanti, Ann Cagnolatti and Chester Pichon, stand with the rest of the court during the krewe's inaugural ball. (Photograph by Milton Pierre)

Queen Mother for the Krewe of Ashanti, Ann Cagnolatti, rolls during its maiden voyage in 1993. (Photograph by Milton Pierre)

The first Ashanti king, Chester Pichon, in 1993 shows off his full costume and scepter. (Photograph by Milton Pierre)

Alvarez Brown enters the 1995 coronation ball as king of the Krewe of Ashanti. (Photograph by Milton Pierre)

A maid of Ashanti greets the crowd during the parade of 1993. (Photograph by Milton Pierre)

A maid of Ashanti greets the crowd during the krewe's inaugural parade. (Photograph by Milton Pierre)

The captain for the Krewe of Ashanti poses for photos with their mother and aunt during the krewe's inaugural ball. (Photograph by Milton Pierre)

Rene Pierre displays his full Ashanti captain costume in 1993. (Photograph by Milton Pierre)

Captain for the Krewe of Ashanti, Rene Pierre, at the krewe's second parade in 1994. (Photograph by Milton Pierre)

A duke for the Krewe of Ashanti is presented during the inaugural coronation ball of 1993. (Photograph by Milton Pierre)

Ashanti duke Frank Robertson at the krewe's first ball in 1993. (Photograph by Rene Pierre)

The Kumboula drum corps performs during the 1993 inaugural ball for the Krewe of Ashanti. (Photograph by Rene Pierre)

Crowned king of Ashanti, Rene Pierre, poses with Victoria Rowell in 1995. (Photograph by Milton Pierre)

The second float in the inaugural parade for the Krewe of Ashanti in 1993. (Photograph by Milton Pierre)

A Zulu king named Oscar Piper and other Zulu officials were invited to the first Ashanti ball. They were so impressed at what they saw, they brought it back to their organization and decided to utilize it themselves. It was a dream for me to put that parade on with a handful of good neighbors who wanted to join in the fun. As the krewe grew fast with outsiders, so did the loss of control. Sadly enough, the krewe suffered a loss in membership as other members opted to stray and form their own clubs. The Krewe of NOMTOC however, has seen major growth as it has become a superkrewe over the last ten years. Gone are the small single decked floats of NOMTOC. This organization boasts a membership of over 1,900 riders on huge superfloats. This West Bank parade has become a pre-Mardi Gras spectacle.

The West Bank citizens plan a whole-day event for this fun krewe. Its parade runs through an African American neighborhood in Algiers. It is definitely one of the best clubs of the West Bank and certainly the biggest. The neighborhood in which it rolls through has a strong community support and following. Those citizens in particular make a big deal out of parade day for NOMTOC. They gather very early under the Crescent City Connection (formerly known as the Greater New Orleans or GNO Bridge), on front lawns of homes, neutral grounds, balconies, and parking lots just to assume a prime spot for viewing and enjoyment. It is an exciting atmosphere and feels much like Mardi Gras itself. For most of the older folk, that is their Fat Tuesday as many of them may not be able to travel to the East Bank for those activities. Most of the families in the Algiers area host large parties and picnics on the day of NOMTOC to celebrate long after the parade has passed.

The NOMTOC group was started in the early '70s by a group of black male educators. I can remember my mother bringing my brother and me to their first parade. It was the most thrilling event, as I watched and listened to the Southern University marching band come storming through the street. My mother worked at Murray Henderson Elementary School at the time and had many colleagues as friends who invited us to their homes for parties to celebrate the day. I'll never forget that experience. As the word spread like wildfire throughout the community, interest sparked and caused a spike in membership. NOMTOC literally went from 200 to 1,000 members almost overnight. It has managed to keep its popularity and pizzazz! There is a lot to look forward to from this krewe. Sadly, they lost a group of their leaders just before the 2011 Carnival season. Warren Green, one of the board members, passed within days of the parade. He was well honored as he should have been.

The NOMTOC ball is also a lot to talk about. Their ball usually happens two weeks before the parade and is held in one of the ballrooms of the Morial Convention Center. This event is colorful and festive. The royal court is presented in grand fashion in an effort to introduce their maids for the year, along with the king and queen. With great food and music, the NOMTOC ball is a must-see event!

The new Krewe of Athena, founded in 2014 and rolling in March of 2015, made history in Metairie with no opposition. It is the first krewe to be created of mainly African American women. The captain, New Orleans native and Orleans Parish high-school administrator Dr. Tamisha Payne, has cited that she was interested in belonging to an organization that was made up of more women that looked like her. However, it was not her main intent. She wanted to use the large platform of Mardi Gras to do positive things for the community. She simply wants to celebrate womanhood on many fronts. Within months, she found herself to be the leader of a fast growing fledgling bunch eager to parade.

It was only a matter of time before she had a lofty amount of women boarding floats with tons of throws and powerhouse bands blowing music that can be heard on Transcontinental Boulevard. Tamisha said she invites growth, but not too fast. She claims that growing too fast can be a bad thing. Losing control is a major concern when large numbers are sprouting more than you can plan for. It would challenge the current administration to alter venues for celebrations and order larger floats and perhaps more floats. She also said that there were initial concerns of crowd response as it pertains to safety. Local parish officials assured her that their krewe would have no trouble and the club's safety would be well intact. She said that the crowds welcomed her and her group with applause and overwhelming joy. The Athena krewe is sure to become an icon of Mardi Gras.

The logo for Krewe of Athena bears the image of the Greek goddess that the krewe chose for its namesake. (Photograph by Rene Pierre)

The queen and king of Athena are presented at the ball. (Photographer unknown)

The 2015 Krewe of Athena's invitation for the inaugural coronation ball. (Photographer unknown)

The king of Athena greets partygoers during the ball. (Photographer unknown)

Debutantes of the royal court gather before the Krewe of Athena's ball.
(Photographer unknown)

A Krewe of Athena grace makes her rounds during the presentation of the court.
(Photographer unknown)

*During the presentation of the court, a grace for the Krewe of Athena spreads joy,
cheer, and mirth.* (Photographer unknown)

Krewe of Athena's captain, right, with a friend at the inaugural ball in 2015.
(Photographer unknown)

The first crowned Queen Athena, Ayanna Fultz, on her royal float. (Photograph by Rene Pierre)

Members of the Krewe of Athena prepare to roll. (Photograph by Rene Pierre)

A member for the royal court of the Krewe of Athena gracefully shows off her costume atop a float. (Photograph by Rene Pierre)

Members of the Krewe of Athena pose for photos before the parade. (Photograph by Rene Pierre)

An officer for the Krewe of Athena poses for a photo before the parade. (Photograph by Rene Pierre)

Ladies of the Krewe of Athena aboard their float before the parade officially begins. (Photograph by Rene Pierre)

Two members of the Krewe of Athena's court pose for a photo on a float. (Photograph by Rene Pierre)

Officers for the Krewe of Athena pose for photos before the parade. (Photograph by Rene Pierre)

Greetings from a maid of Athena. (Photograph by Rene Pierre)

The Mystic Krewe of Femme Fatale is yet another welcoming women's club made of African Americans. They too made history in 2014 by presenting their inaugural parade in uptown New Orleans. While much is not known about this new organization, it did put on a nice parade. The ladies seemed to have had a great time. The city is looking forward to extraordinary things from this group. It is understood that the Kern family has the current contract for the floats. Their krewe colors are candy apple red, black, and white. Their signature throw is the designer ladies compact. Its first queen was Gwendolyn Rainey.

CHAPTER 4

BEHIND THE SCENES

In other areas of Mardi Gras, African Americans have persevered. They were always a part of the support systems that make Mardi Gras thrive. Many of the older krewes have been known to hire black female seamstresses to sew costumes for kings, queens, and other royalty. They have also been instrumental in acting as valet to assist royalty get dress for the big parade. They have also taken on roles as make-up artists, riding assistants, chauffeurs, and—the most honorable of all—*artist!*

Many citizens are unaware that most of the major float builders hire African Americans to put detailed images on those beautiful floats. It is true and evident that these float builders have recognized and respected the ornate and fine art of several local artists who happen to be African American. Among the lineup of artists in the New Orleans area are the best: Raymond Bouie, Reynard Rochon Jr., Damon Bouie, and me (Rene Pierre), working in dens throughout the metro area. The absolute best float artist in all of Mardi Gras, known for his illustrious storybook style, is New Orleanian Raymond Bouie.

Raymond has the honor and privilege of painting for the krewes of Rex, Orpheus, parts of Endymion, and Hermes. Raymond has a long history of painting experience. Raymond, in the early '80s, painted floats for the Barth Brothers who were famous for introducing the self-propelled floats and the front gates to the World's Fair of 1984. Soon after, he began painting for Blaine Kern Companies. There he joined greats like Joe Ory in painting the Bacchus and Alla parades.

Renowned artist Raymond Bouie teaches a group of students techniques used to paint floats in 2004. (Photograph by Rene Pierre)

A Mardi Gras artist and Mardi Gras Signature School students from L. E. Rabouin in front of a float. Students were able to meet and learn from actual artists involved with Carnival preparations. (Photograph by Rene Pierre)

Rene Pierre with one of his Mardi Gras papier-mâché creations in 1997. (Photographer unknown)

An artist paints a mural. (Photograph by Rene Pierre)

A Mardi Gras artist working on float construction. (Photograph by Rene Pierre)

An artist continues work on a mural. (Photograph by Rene Pierre)

An artist adds the finishing touches to a jester's head for the Krewe of Comogo in Plaquemine, Louisiana. (Photograph by Rene Pierre)

A student at the Mardi Gras Signature School works on the finer details of a float. (Photograph by Rene Pierre)

A float fabricator works on the last stages of constructing a float. (Photograph by Rene Pierre)

Mardi Gras artist Rene Pierre puts the final layer of paint on a float preparing it for the Carnival season. (Photograph by Quincy Howard Sr.)

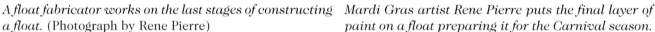

 Damon Bouie, the nephew of Raymond, is a float designer. He is talented and steeped in graphic art styles. His works remain to be some of the top in its genre. Rochon is a newcomer compared to the older giants. Mr. Rochon, the son of the late Reynard Rochon Sr. of the Dutch Morial administration, got his start in the convention decorating industry then transferred to the float building business. I was afforded the opportunity to become educated with the younger Reynard at Xavier University of Louisiana in the early '90s. We majored in art together under the leadership of the late Charles Graves and John Scott who passed shortly after Katrina. Reynard painted floats for the Krewe of D'Etat then later moved to the Kern Companies. He was always a great and innovative artist. Ricco Rideaux was an amateur at the time, who started shortly after I was hired at Cantrell & Sons in 1996. Ricco is a very young aspiring artist who is now selling his art in Jackson Square.

 While there are many great artists working in other dens and studios to produce the beauty of Mardi Gras, the aforementioned group is given special recognition due to the nature of this book. However, I must give

Some tools of the Mardi Gras artistry trade—gallons of paint and a paint sprayer. (Photograph by Rene Pierre)

Rene Pierre with some of the final pieces needed to finish a Frozen *inspired float.* (Photographer unknown)

a "hats off" to all artists who help make Mardi Gras a moving art show. Further, after a brief interview with Raymond Bouie, he demands that every artists is always in the process of learning new techniques. He says we discover something new every day and that there is no such thing as anyone stealing a style or a stroke. He says all of us learned from the world's greatest like Raphael, da Vinci, Michelangelo, and van Gogh. Artists learn from other artists then add their own touch.

In my own career, I've had the privilege to train and mentor young people from several local area high schools. After noticing young energetic talent, I chose them to become apprentices, knowing that their exposure to the Mardi Gras industry was minimal. These young men and women would never have been able to pierce into this industry if I hadn't had a chance to introduce them to it. There is always room for new budding artists to take part in this lucrative industry. Because our students are born into such a culture, they understand the celebration but not necessarily the preparation phase.

Mardi Gras Signature School students, Terell Poiree and Nathaniel Joiner, get an up-close look at a float. Terell and Nathaniel were some of the first students of the Signature School. (Photograph by Rene Pierre)

Float created by Louisiana rental company PFJ Floats. (Photograph by Rene Pierre)

Student Tyree Tucker helps decorate one of many Mardi Gras floats in 2011. Local professional artists offer young artists the opportunity to earn money while learning first-hand how much work goes into Carnival preparation. (Photograph by Rene Pierre)

Blaine Kern and Rene Pierre with art students from L. E. Rabouin High School in 2004. Kern and Pierre are two of the many Mardi Gras artists who volunteer to work with young artists. (Photographer unknown)

The first students of the Mardi New Orleans Signature School get an up-close look at floats in 2004. (Photograph by Rene Pierre)

A student at the Mardi Gras Signature School adds detail to a practice wall in art class. (Photograph by Rene Pierre)

The brainchild of Mr. Anthony Amato, previously superintendent of Orleans Parish schools, developed several schools in the local area in an effort to offer students more options in education. Though some frowned upon his practices, his projects were well intended and were beginning to become fruitful until Hurricane Katrina hit in August of 2005. The Mardi Gras Signature School offered high school juniors and seniors the opportunity to participate in an art program linked to Blaine Kern Artist, Inc. This allowed them to complete half a day of core curriculum at their school and spend the remaining half at the Kern studio learning from me, as the teacher of record, and training as apprentices from the other professionals. These students were treated with much kindness. Those students gained a wealth of experience from the Kern workers.

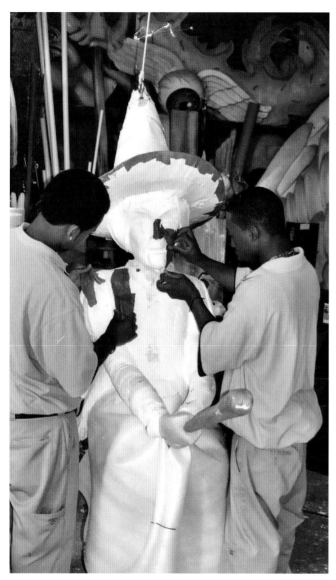

Students help create a prop for the Blaine Kern Artist, Inc. Young artists were able to get a behind-the-scenes look at what it takes to make the artistry of Carnival come to life. (Photograph by Rene Pierre)

Signature School student Nathaniel Joiner works on molding a prop. (Photograph by Rene Pierre)

A student adds color to detailed pieces for a float. (Photograph by Rene Pierre)

Students work on constructing their own miniature float designs. (Photograph by Rene Pierre)

They were able to learn the construction phase as well as decorating. They adorned the Orpheus floats with flowers and gold leafing. They also stretched cloth on new floats, then primed them for artwork. They were also instrumental in putting props in place on the floats. The students had a great time there and claimed it to be the highlight of their academic career. Mr. Tyree Tucker, one of the last to study under that program, still practices his craft with precision. He's become one of the up-and-coming talents that will be sure to gain his place in our industry. His beautiful sketches and paint style improve daily. With more training and practice these students could become the next super-artist of the industry.

Budding young artists from L. E. Rabouin High School on a fieldtrip at the former Algiers location of Mardi Gras World in 2004. (Photograph by Rene Pierre)

Artists work on constructing a papier-mâché snowman prop for a parade.
(Photograph by Rene Pierre)

The finished papier-mâché snowman prop. (Photograph by Rene Pierre)

Mardi Gras artist Rene Pierre works on the early stages of constructing a float. (Photograph by Johnny Winfield)

A papier-mâché teapot prop before it's added to a float. (Photograph by Rene Pierre)

The wooden frame of a Mardi Gras float. (Photograph by Rene Pierre)

A miniature model of the Zulu king's float. (Photograph by Rene Pierre)

Miniature models of parade floats. (Photograph by Rene Pierre)

Float in warehouse depicting an artist's rendition of Jim Carrey's take on the main character from The Mask. (Photographer by Rene Pierre)

A Valentine themed float ready to be hitched and join the parade. (Photograph by Rene Pierre)

A completed birthday themed float is ready for the party of Mardi Gras. (Photograph by Rene Pierre)

Float builder Quincy Howard Sr. reaches new heights as he works on a float.
(Photograph by Rene Pierre)

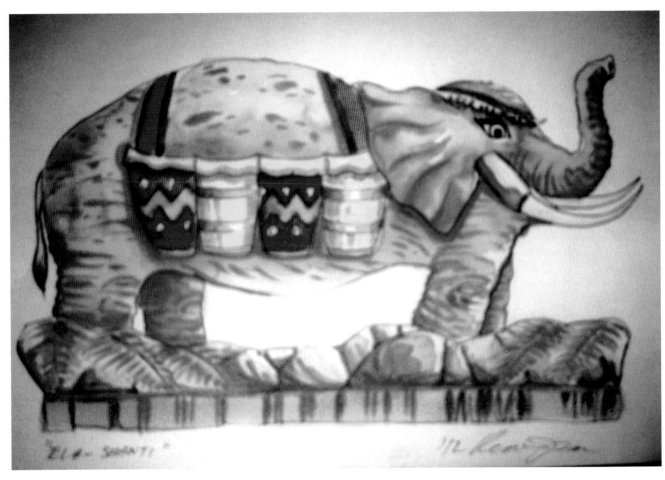

Sketch of an elephant-shaped float. Before a design is built, it must take shape on paper. (Photograph by Rene Pierre)

Sketch of a tortoise-shaped float. Designs may change drastically from the drafting and building stages, but a drawing is a necessary starting point. (Photograph by Rene Pierre)

The same women who made costumes for themselves and their families also played an important role in larger Carnival preparations. It was not uncommon to find these talented African American women sewing in the studios of the elite old-line krewes. Many Creole women worked for the krewes of Comus, Momus, and Rex. This group of women was involved in a special career that didn't offer itself to black people at one time.

Many of the high society balls commissioned these ladies to sew for them. They also sewed for many family clubs, which included truck-float and small neighborhood groups. Often these women started out by sewing wedding dresses for uptown families. Once their talent was discovered, they were offered opportunities to sew for the Carnival clubs. To this day, many of our women still sew for major krewes. It is amazing how everyone has a special place in Mardi Gras. This only shows the dire need to have total participation from all of our talented citizens to create such a fantastic festival.

Float fabricator Johnny Winfield works on a float for Krewe of Comogo in Plaquemine, Louisiana. (Photograph by Rene Pierre)

Muslin cloth covers wooden frame of float. (Photograph by Rene Pierre)

An artist uses a paint sprayer to add detail to a float. (Photograph by Rene Pierre)

Gallons of paint on the floor of a float building warehouse. It takes a lot of paint (and time) to create the detailed images on Mardi Gras floats. (Photograph by Rene Pierre)

Sketch of the "First Wives Club" Zulu float. (Photograph by Rene Pierre)

Artist Rene Pierre works on a Cleopatra float just weeks before the parade. (Photographer unknown)

A completed float for the Krewe of Comogo in Plaquemine, Louisiana, stands in a warehouse. (Photograph by Rene Pierre)

An Egyptian themed float is ready to set sail on the parade route. (Photograph by Rene Pierre)

A float for a member of court sits in a Mardi Gras warehouse full of other float decorations. (Photograph by Rene Pierre)

CHAPTER 5

HOMEMADE MARDI GRAS

There are diehards who still manage to adorn their homemade Mardi Gras garb every year to march through the streets of New Orleans. Neighborhoods like the Farbourg Marigny host parades like the St. Ann Society, which is a large group of native folk who create wonderful handmade costumes to march up and down Esplanade Avenue and Frenchmen Street. Other neighborhoods, like the Tremé area, have their hosts of old Skeleton krewes and Baby Dolls. Even the neighborhood drag queens come out to spark fun with the general Carnival patrons. There is a place for everyone to take part in the liveliest time of the year.

An Indian enjoys some libations as he celebrates Mardi Gras of 1970. (Photograph by Milton Pierre)

A New Orleans Indian's plumage adds an extra dimension as he dances during Mardi Gras in the 1980s. The intricate patterns on Indian costumes are usually done by hand. (Photograph by Milton Pierre)

Moreover, we still get to enjoy the Krewe du Vieux and the Curtis Pierre samba corps. Both groups are large and march only. They do not own floats. They are steeped in the tradition of showing off costumes. Many tourists come here to track down these particular groups for pictures and video coverage to bring back home. In this century, we must remember that technology allows the world to see us party, insomuch that the world longs to become a part of the show. An African American costume guru, Michelle Levine, has been a special part of Mardi Gras for years. This female reveler's face has been on multiple covers of books and magazines published about Carnival. Her beautiful and creative costumes attract people to her. She participates with the St. Ann Society annually. She is a rare and special treat to see.

An Indian won't let his intricate costume get in the way of his interactions with other Mardi Gras revelers in 1969. (Photograph by Milton Pierre)

Before these new groups formed, the Tremé parade had a special place in Mardi Gras known for its homemade parade. During the '70s the Tremé parade was a direct evolution of the community centers involvement with senior citizens and children. The parade that then traveled through the official Tremé neighborhood consisted of handcrafted floats built on the backs of pickup trucks and car trailers, local dance schools, and some of the best marching bands from local predominately African American schools. This parade was usually held during the weekend before the official parading season would begin downtown. It was surely a vibrant way to kick off the Carnival season. Everyone couldn't wait until the big parades started after the Tremé parade passed. There hasn't been much talk of resurrecting the Tremé Tambourine and Fans organization, but it would be a welcomed return.

Tambourine and Fans started as a protest group spear headed by Jerome "Duck" Smith. Their initial claim to fame was protesting the erection of the I-10 over N. Claiborne Avenue. It's understood that this project in particular was the direct cause of the local businesses along that street losing revenue and, in some cases, going out of business. Smith was very upset at this. He was already known in the community as a civil rights leader. Ironically, he never meant for the protest to evolve into a Super Sunday festival. To this day he ensures that didn't happen, and the two events have nothing to do with each other. There are even more African American organizations in the midst of evolving from all walks of life and backgrounds.

CHAPTER 6

MARCHING TO A NEW BEAT

The first Mardi Gras parades saw very little school-band participation. In fact, parades were mostly accompanied by brass bands and military units. The high schools really didn't become fully engaged until the turn of century. The '40s and '50s brought on more involvement from high school bands as parades became larger and grew in number. As floats began to change their dynamics and parades expanded in length, it was only natural for high schools to be invited to take part in the revelry. However, African American bands didn't participate in major Mardi Gras parades until the dust settled on all of the civil rights activities.

Dejan's Olympia Brass Band escorts the Zulu Tramps during the krewe's 1989 parade. Before school bands were a feature of parades, krewes of the past were mostly joined by brass and military groups. (Photograph by Milton Pierre)

Two Mardi Gras icons occupy the same space as a five-piece band plays in front of a painting of flambeaux men. (Photograph by Rene Pierre)

As the '60s came to an end, the tolerance for change and the ease of tension from the movement witnessed African American high-school bands being invited to march in all-white parades. The unique sound and boisterous style of these school bands started an era of electrifying music that set new standards for parading in Mardi Gras. The black population of New Orleans grew rapidly and since schools were integrating, there was no surprised that this phenomenon would occur. As the Orleans Parish school district expanded, so did the music programs. It wasn't long before they all were in high demand.

These high-school and middle-school programs brought on a new feeling of parades with their thunderous beats from bass drums and effervescent dancers. The tone of Mardi Gras in New Orleans is now changed forever. The larger krewes like Bacchus and Endymion really gave these kids their first chance to march. To the students, it was like being a superstar for one night. The schools spent plenty of money on uniforms and costumes for the girls. The dancing girls went from knit dresses to sparkling sequin bodysuits. The schools bought into this Mardi Gras thing and saw it as an opportunity to earn the extra cash needed to operate their music programs and keep updated uniforms for a continued fresh look.

The larger high schools began to become powerhouses in their own right. The only private school that saw themselves competing with public schools was St. Augustine High School. An all-boys catholic school located in the Seventh Ward of New Orleans. Their striking sound and slick moves made them popular very fast. The notable purple and gold uniforms were so different from the other schools, you couldn't help but to quickly identify them as the band came down the street. Their legendary director, Edwin Hampton, coined a name for himself in catapulting this school into a Mardi Gras staple. They have marched in parades nationwide. They have had the pleasure of even traveling to New York to march in the Macy's Thanksgiving Day Parade more than once. Other high schools were just as good—and some even better—during those decades of old.

The St. Augustine High School band gets ready to put on a show for the crowd at the Ashanti parade of 1993. School bands—of all grades—have become a welcomed musical addition during Mardi Gras. (Photograph by Rene Pierre)

The St. Augustine High School marching band puts on a show during the Krewe of Zulu parade in 2002. (Photograph by Rene Pierre)

John F. Kennedy High School was a force to be reckoned with. They were among all the other popular Orleans Parish school bands like Alcee Fortier, John McDonogh, and McDonogh #35 high schools, who are still performing at stellar rates. Warren Easton, G. W. Carver, and L. B. Landry were also among the best high schools, taking home several trophies that upset a lot of the competition. Other bands of note include those from Edna Karr, Marion Abramson, Joseph S. Clark, Booker T. Washington, O. Perry Walker, West Jefferson, Francis T. Nicholls, and Alfred Lawless high schools; F. W. Gregory, Edward Phillips, McDonogh #28, and Pierre Capdau junior high schools; and Samuel J. Green elementary school.

Big sound comes from the band of Abramson High School as they march in 2000.
(Photograph by Rene Pierre)

The Abramson High School majorettes before they march in a 2000 parade.
(Photograph by Rene Pierre)

The Abramson High School band stays in step during the 2002 Zulu parade.
(Photograph by MIlton Pierre)

The John F. Kennedy High School band stays in step during the 1989 Zulu parade. (Photograph by Milton Pierre)

In addition to our public school bands, the all-girl high school bands of St. Mary's Academy and Xavier Preparatory contributed to the celebration with a big bang and big competition. These girls came to the game bringing it. They gave stellar performances that created much talk among the community. Their bands, too, became a mainstay in Mardi Gras.

The African American school bands were also famous for competing for trophies. The infamous Krewe of Freret—the original one—was notorious for staging band contests within their parade. This attracted all of the big powerhouse bands to be anxious to march for them. Because of where that parade started at the corner of Freret and Nashville streets, the Alcee Fortier High School band would make a grand entrance into the parade from their school building.

The Freret parade created such a following that it induced major safety concerns among the police department. They were afraid that the revelers following the bands would cause havoc. In some instances they did. The younger students were also putting in the time and work, which resulted in them sounding like they were in high school. They would come from schools all over the city, joining parades in the colors of Carter G. Woodson Middle, Walter L. Cohen High, Kohn Middle, and Andrew J. Bell Junior High. More recently Sophie B. Wright and McMain Secondary (with its seventh- and eight-grade students) schools have joined the festivities around 2002.

Newer charter schools—some of which were created after Hurricane Katrina—that march with exhilarating sound and performances are Lake Area New Tech High, Dr. Martin Luther King Middle, Fannie C. Williams Charter, Miller-McCoy Academy, Paul Habans, James Singleton, and Milestone Sabis. Some schools may have been omitted due to name changes after Hurricane Katrina. Others became defunct after closing due to low budgets, underperforming test scores, and other problems. However, the fabric of Mardi Gras parades has been forever changed because of what predominantly African American schools have contributed over the years. It can only get better as all of them are constantly looking for the next best thing.

The Southern University band marches with the Krewe of Zulu in 1989. (Photograph by Rene Pierre)

Providing a beat and entertainment in 1989, the Southern University band marches along with Zulu. (Photograph by Rene Pierre)

CHAPTER 7

A NEW FACE OF FLOAT RIDERS

What had long been a segregated tradition exclusive to only the white community, slowly evolved into a fun occasion for nearly everyone. Largely, Mardi Gras parades were reserved for mainly white organizations, that, in those days, had chosen to keep it that way. With the exception of Zulu, blacks had no other options outside of using neighborhood truck floats to ride. However, as decades passed, newer generations of whites became more tolerant of change. There was also an immersion of newly college-educated African Americans, who earned much higher salaries than their parents, thus affording them wider options to ride in large wealthy organizations. With that notion, people of color were permitted to apply for membership in white-owned organizations.

For some krewes, it was a welcoming event. Others were not so accepting. This was a frustrating time for New Orleanians. The old-line krewes chose to fight a new law spearheaded by the late Dorothy Mae Taylor. Taylor was a member of the New Orleans City Council in the early 1990s. The law was written in an effort to prevent discrimination by white Carnival krewes. Though not all white-owned krewes practiced discriminatory action. The Krewe of Endymion has always had black krewe members, unbeknownst to the public. So did some of the smaller krewes. The krewes of Pontchartrain, Minerva, and Tucks opened their membership ranks as a congenial effort to be inclusive. This took place long before what became referred to as "Taylor's Law," which was enacted in 1992.

Crowned King Bacchus Anthony Mackie greets the crowd in 2016. New Orleans native Mackie was the first black king for the Krewe of Bacchus. (Photograph by Elon Photography Inc.)

King Endymion
George Byron LaFargue, Jr.

IS COMMANDING YOUR PRESENCE AT A

ROYAL RECEPTION

AS MONARCH OF THE

2012 ENDYMION EXTRAVAGANZA

ON SUNDAY, THE TWELFTH OF FEBRUARY

TWO THOUSAND AND TWELVE

AT SIX O'CLOCK IN THE EVENING

THE SHOW VENUE

1755 TCHOUPITOULAS STREET

NEW ORLEANS, LOUISIANA

An invitation to Endymion's 2012 ball with the krewe's first black king, George LaFargue Jr. (Photograph by Rene Pierre)

Members of the Krewe of Endymion gather for a photo before it's time for the floats to roll. Black members—hidden behind masks like the other members—have always had a place in the predominantly-white krewe. (Photograph by Rene Pierre)

Dressed to the nines, in 2007 the first black king and queen of the Krewe of King Arthur pose for photos. (Photograph by Milton Pierre)

The second crowned black king, Patrick Clementine, during the 2005 coronation ball for the Krewe of King Arthur. (Photograph by Rene Pierre)

The second black king of the Krewe of King Arthur, Patrick Clementine, with Gaynell Chopfield. (Photograph by Rene Pierre)

King Arthur and Queen Guinevere are presented during the coronation ball for the Krewe of King Arthur. (Photograph by Rene Pierre)

Some of the first black members of the Krewe of King Arthur gather for a photo before boarding the floats for the parade of 2001. (Photograph by Milton Pierre)

Krewe members of King Arthur pose for a photo on a float for the 2003 parade. (Photograph by Rene Pierre)

The first black Merlin for the Krewe of King Arthur, Patrick Clementine, greets the crowd during the 2005 parade. (Photograph by Rene Pierre)

Merlin for the Krewe of King Arthur, Patrick Clementine, with his assistant and brother, Ralph Clementine. (Photograph by Rene Pierre)

Merlin for the Krewe of King Arthur Patrick Clementine with Rene Pierre.
(Photographer unknown)

Morganna and Merlin pose for photos before the Krewe of King Arthur's parade.
(Photograph by Rene Pierre)

The young Krewe of Orpheus publically announced its intention to be
inclusive in 1993. Harry Connick Jr., a founding member, appeared on
television to clearly state that the krewe was opened to all who wished
to participate. Some members may have squawked or even jumped
ship, but for the most part white-owned krewes remained together and
enjoyed good times. The Orpheus Krewe is a favorite superkrewe among
New Orleans Mardi Gras krewes. While some krewes chose to opt out
of integrating and fold, others simply chose to no longer ride on their
floats. The latter continue to host their Carnival balls and other annual
activities. The remaining, unmentioned ones chose to keep quiet about
their organizations' changes.

Black members of the predominantly white Krewe of Orpheus before the 2007 parade. (Photograph by Rene Pierre)

Not all parade krewes are big-headed, but few can make the papier-mâché costume toppers work like the members of Orpheus. (Photograph by Rene Pierre)

A Mardi Gras float before it takes to the streets depicts a child's birthday party. The krewes may have taken longer to integrate but many of city's people already seemed to know how to celebrate together. (Photograph by Rene Pierre)

Flambeaux carriers for Orpheus are inspected before lighting the parade route in 1998. (Photograph by Rene Pierre)

With the rise of new krewes appearing in the '70s and '80s, more African Americans were joining integrated Mardi Gras organizations. Soon, all of the superkrewes were significantly integrated. The primary color of Mardi Gras had become green. If one can afford it, one can ride. Presently, Endymion and Orpheus hold the largest number of African American members of the white-owned krewes. There is also rumor that the Krewe of Rex includes a few famous, noteworthy African Americans. Whatever it may be, the New Orleans krewes have come of age. And, it has been a very inclusive decade all around, on nearly all fronts.

CHAPTER 8

INTERVIEWS

PATRICK CLEMENTINE

King Arthur XXXI, 2008
Krewe's second African American king

Rene: Did you know you were going to be king?

Patrick: No, in April of that year, I was approached by the captain who asked me to be king. I was surprised. A group conversation conjured up the idea.

Rene: How did you feel when it was announced?

Patrick: Awesome! That's when I knew it was going to be a reality. I had always felt that it was unreal up until that point.

Rene: What was your entire day like?

Patrick: I woke up with my eyes to

King of the Krewe of King Arthur Patrick Clementine with his sword Excalibur during the krewe's ball. (Photograph by Rene Pierre)

the ceiling and thought to myself, "I'm going to be king." That morning was consumed with family, of course. There was toasting before the limos arrived. Then, I was escorted to the formation area. I couldn't believe the traffic was being held back for me. Arriving to the floats was exciting! I got out of the limo as King XXXI. I felt surreal at the moment. The marching bands were warming up on the neutral ground [and] added to the electric atmosphere. I was elated.

Rene: Would you do it again?

Patrick: No, only because it could never be duplicated. The first experience is always bliss. I'd rather have that first memory forever.

GEORGE LAFARGUE
King Endymion, 2012
Krewe's first African American king

Rene: What made you want to join the Endymion organization?

George: I started as a substitute rider for a friend and enjoyed the ride so much—especially the entrance to the Superdome—that I decided to stay with it.

Rene: When did you officially join?

George: Two thousand five.

Rene: How were you received as a member?

George: Many members that I bumped into were already friends of mine and they were surprised to see me. One of my older friends cried after they learned I was chosen as king.

Rene: How did you feel when the captain announced that you had won the prestigious role as king?

George: At that moment I felt like I'd won the lottery big time! But I didn't hear the first announcement because they called out a member number not a name. On returning from a restroom visit, I heard my name called in conjunction with the member number. I saw my wife as she screamed and tears began to fall. Everyone gathered around me to congratulate me. It was very exciting! I wasn't expecting it.

Rene: What was your most memorable moment during your reign as king?

George: On parade night, when krewe officials costumed me on the float before entering the Superdome. Because of the earlier rains in the night, I couldn't wear the entire outfit along the route so they suited me up right before the float headed for the entrance. As my float entered the Dome, the house lights went out and a spotlight shined on me. Then, the float stopped in front of the table where my wife and mother were seated. It was a wonderful feeling. As the tears rolled down my face, I thought of my deceased father and thought of how he would have loved this.

Rene: Were you disappointed in the weather and did you enjoy the ride anyway?

George: As being selected as king, I didn't know there was a Catholic Mass held at the dressing center for its members. The late Monsignor [Clinton] Doskey approached me shortly after the Mass and comforted me by expressing how he'd prayed to God about me. He reassured that I would be fine and that the weather would hold off and I personally would not experience any conflict.

Rene: How did the crowd along the parade route respond to you?

George: Tremendous! The people came to see a phenomenon. One older lady and her husband on Canal Street, in front of the old Cox Cable building, came up to the float to tell me they came just to see me. The lady specifically said, "I haven't been to a parade in fifty years but I weathered the storm just to see you, if I never see it again." That made my night.

Rene: What did your reign do for the ethnical disposition of the organization?

George: Most of Endymion's members already understood the selection process of its king and knew that this moment could have happened much earlier in the krewe's lifespan as African Americans belonged to the organization for two decades but in small doses. There is even proof that they belonged to the krewe shortly after its inception. I thought the opportunity was fair.

Rene: Would you reign again if you could or would you pass it along to the second chosen envelope?

George: That's a very difficult question, Rene. But I couldn't pass it up for nothing in the world. I think this is a trick question.

George Lafargue, crowned first black king of the superkrewe Endymion. (Photographer unknown, courtesy of George Lafargue)

LARON QUINN NELSON
Costume designer
Krewe of Athena's first king, 2015

Rene: How did you get started?

Laron: Well, I did a headpiece for a pageant in 2006. Once I did that one, other people took notice and word spread fast. I started doing more of them. This also inspired the birth of my organization, the Krewe of Symphony.

Rene: What did it take for you to land a large krewe?

Laron: I started to do costumes for the dukes of Zulu, but only the headpieces, suits, and boots. But when the word spread about my collar work, I was able to do costumes for Mr. Big Shot and Mr. Big Stuff and some walking warriors for the Zulu organization.

Rene: Where do you see yourself five years from now?

Laron: I would like to start my own parading krewe—the Krewe of Symphony. I would like to costume the entire parade and grow the business.

Rene: Where do you get your ideas for designs?

Laron: Clients come to me with ideas. Then I draw sketches of some of those ideas. Some ideas and styles come from other designers as well.

Rene: Did you know that you were going to be king?

Laron: Yes, I did. I was commissioned to create their costumes and as we discussed costumes I mentioned that someday I wouldn't mind being king in the future. A few days later the leaders asked would I consider being their king now. I was surprised, but I said yes. I was elated. I accepted graciously.

Rene: How did it feel to be the first king? What was it like when the float started moving through the streets?

Laron: Well, let's go back to the ball. It was awesome! At first, I aspired to be King Zulu. But as I started getting into working with them, [I] realized it wouldn't happen. It was definitely a great experience with Athena. It was a thrill of a lifetime!

Rene: What was your parade day like from beginning to end?

Laron: Believe it or not, I did what most kings wouldn't do. I worked earlier that day because I still had costumes to complete for other krewes. However, by mid-day my house was full of krewe members and family all excited about what the night would bring.

We were loading the U-Haul truck with costumes and throws. The limos came to pick us up. We were then escorted to Clearview Mall where there was a prepared party hosted in the mall inside of a special ballroom. A brass band escorted us to the floats.

Rene: So this room acted as a krewe headquarters of sort?

Laron: Yes, it is used by all of the Metairie krewes to prep for float riding.

Rene: Sounds like fun.

Laron: Yes, it was.

Rene: Was it what you expected?

Laron: It was more than what I expected! People were very welcoming. We had no problems. We were so happy, man. So much was going on that night. There were other krewes holding up signs of love and support. Spectators were shouting "Thank you for coming!" and "Thanks for bringing the funk to Metairie!"

Rene: Did you anticipate any discrimination?

Laron: No. They were very receptive. They got into it. The crowds were looking forward to the double header that night.

Rene: Do you think there's a paradigm shift among women in Mardi Gras?

Laron: Yes. This year really was a progressive time for that. Everyone wants to participate in Mardi Gras to some extent. Historically there wasn't much room for women on floats due to the number of all-male organizations. So it's no surprise that more women organizations are sprouting up. Even the onset of Mystic Krewe of Femme Fatale was a great first-year effort. I think there's plenty room for women to do their thing.

Rene: Do you see Athena growing fast?

Laron: Yes, sir! I think if they stay within their limits and continue to do quality over quantity, they are going to grow.

Rene: Well, congratulations to you on your reign as king. I know you are going to help this club become a spectacular event. This will be a good thing.

The first king, Laron Nelson, for the Krewe of Athena stands before his luminous and bejeweled collar. (Photograph by Rene Pierre)

GERARD "BO" DOLLIS JR.
Chief of the Wild Magnolias tribe

Rene: When did you know you wanted to follow in your father's footsteps?

Bo Jr.: At age six, I used to look at my dad sew his aprons and patches in our living room. That's when I realized I wanted to do this. Me and my mom used to follow my dad in our van during all of the marches to support tribe members who would get tired or overheated in the heavy costumes. At first my mom was against me masking because of the violent behavior that could occur during marches. Anyway, I took two of my mom's outdated purses and cut them up for the beads that were on them and began to sew my own patches. My dad also had a can of beads that I used to gather beads from and sew with. I learned how to bead at the age of eight.

Rene: When did your dad ask you to perform with his band?

Bo Jr.: I was about six years old and he put a microphone in front of me at Jazz Fest and gave me a tambourine to beat. By the time I made twelve, I started to travel internationally with his band. It was a challenge with school but I still went. My first trip abroad was Osaka, Japan. It was a weeklong tour. I learned a lot being so young and it made me grow up fast! After seeing starving children in Mexico it was an eye-opener for me. I learned from my grandfather, too, who was Harold Dejean of the Olympia Brass Band.

Rene: Where did you attend high school?

Bo Jr.: I went to Warren Easton for one year, then finished my last years at Walter L. Cohen not far from our house.

Rene: Did you entertain your peers at school?

Bo Jr.: Yes. It was an assembly for Black History Month. A lot of students were shocked to know that I can sing. I became Mr. Popular overnight.

Rene: What color was your first suit?

Bo Jr.: Yellow with rainbow tips.

Rene: How long does it take to sew a new suit for the next Mardi Gras?

Bo Jr.: Three hundred sixty-five days, period!

Rene: What do you believe was your best suit?

Bo Jr.: My black suit of 2016. It honored my dad and other chiefs who passed. All of them were father figures to me besides my dad.

Rene: Has being an Indian granted you the magnitude of fame that you wear today?

Bo Jr.: Yes, it has. I started getting calls to do commercials for attorneys and other organizations. I'm filming another one for the Saints football season. I've been making suits for thirty years and look forward to passing on this tradition to my sons.

Rene: What is the average cost of a New Orleans Indian suit?

Bo Jr.: Between $3,000 and $5,000. Nowadays, we hold fundraisers to help members purchase the more expensive items like the feathers and plumes, especially.

Rene: How to become a New Orleans Indian?

Bo Jr.: For our tribe we give potential members a test. I ask them to sew a small patch. And if they finish it in a reasonable time, I know that they're sincere and dedicated. It shows loyalty and readiness. Then, I give them a bigger one like an apron. If they finish that, I know they're ready. At that point they have to be at every practice every Sunday to learn the culture of traditions through song, language, signals, and history.

Bo Dollis Jr., in 2018, prepares his costume for the next Mardi Gras season. (Photograph by Rene Pierre)

A young Gerard "Bo" Dollis Jr. masking with his father, the late Bo Dollis Sr., downtown for Super Sunday in 1991. (Photographer unknown, photo courtesy of Gerard "Bo" Dollis Jr.)

AFTERWORD

I hope that you've enjoyed this work on the roots of African Americans' involvement in Mardi Gras—New Orleans style. From Zulu to the Indians, there is so much more to know and discover. The vivid stories of yesteryear and the future of Carnival are always interesting. This is especially true for the history buff who wants to know where and how things got started. The old saying is, "You don't know where you're going until you know where you've come from" rings true.

"I know you Mardi Gras!"

INDEX